AWESTRUCK

A JOURNAL
FOR FINDING AWE
YEAR-ROUND

WILLIAM MORROW

AN IMPRINT OF HARPERCOLLINS*PUBLISHERS*

AWESTRUCK: A JOURNAL FOR FINDING AWE YEAR-ROUND

Copyright © 2018 by William Morrow. All rights reserved.

Printed in China. No part of this book may be used or reproduced in any

manner whatsoever without written permission except in the case of

brief quotations embodied in critical articles and reviews.

For information, address HarperCollins Publishers,

195 Broadway, New York, NY 10007.

HarperCollins books may be purchased for educational, business, or sales

promotional use. For information, please email the Special Markets Department at

SPsales@harpercollins.com.

FIRST EDITION

Designed by Lise Sukhu

Text by R. C. Patrizio

Library of Congress Cataloging-in-Publication Data has been applied for.

ISBN 978-0-06-279774-2

18 19 20 21 22   IM   10 9 8 7 6 5 4 3 2 1

HELLO, YOU!

YOU'VE STUMBLED UPON SOMETHING SLIGHTLY MAGICAL, A LITTLE INTANGIBLE, AND POTENTIALLY TRANSFORMATIVE: A JOURNAL.

A LILY PAD WHERE YOU CAN BE YOURSELF: TRUE BLUE, BITTER AS HELL, ANXIOUS, AWAKE (WOKE!), ELECTRIFIED, MYSTIFIED, ILLUMINATED, HAPPY, OR HUNGRY.

YOU KNOW THAT LINE WHEN MISSY ELLIOTT GOES, "BREAK ME OFF / SHOW ME WHAT YOU GOT?" / THAT'S WHAT I'M TALKING ABOUT.

THERE'S A PROMPT FOR EACH DAY OF THE YEAR TO TICKLE YOUR SENSES AND DRAW OUT YOUR INTUITIONS. FIND THE SEASON YOU'RE IN AND START JOURNALING.

THIS IS AN EXERCISE IN CONNECTION, FEAR, HONESTY, AND BEAUTY. IT'S MOSTLY ABOUT KEEPING IT REAL, THOUGH.

KEEP THIS SOMEWHERE SAFE—WHERE YOU CAN BE YOU—TO EXPLORE THE INTRICA-CIES OF YOUR OWN HEART AND MIND, AND THE WORLD AROUND YOU.

HELENA BONHAM CARTER ONCE SAID: "I THINK EVERYTHING IN LIFE IS ART. WHAT YOU DO. HOW YOU DRESS. THE WAY YOU LOVE SOMEONE, AND HOW YOU TALK. YOUR SMILE AND YOUR PERSONALITY. WHAT YOU BELIEVE IN, AND ALL YOUR DREAMS. THE WAY YOU DRINK YOUR TEA. HOW YOU DECORATE YOUR HOME. OR PARTY. YOUR GROCERY LIST. THE FOOD YOU MAKE. HOW YOUR WRITING LOOKS. AND THE WAY YOU FEEL. LIFE IS ART."

THIS IS YOUR STORY, YOUR POINT OF VIEW. AND IT IS ART. HOW MUCH ARE YOU WILLING TO REVEAL?

IT'LL TAKE 365 DAYS (AND A LIFETIME) TO FIND OUT.

WITH LOVE,
RCP

DATE: ___/___/20___

TODAY, YOU'RE THE CREATIVE DIRECTOR OF YOUR OWN LIFE.

WHAT DOES YOUR "STRATEGIC REBRAND" LOOK LIKE?
HOW DO YOU CHANGE YOUR ATTITUDE, YOUR STYLE, YOUR
OPINIONS, OR YOUR BEHAVIORS TO MAKE YOURSELF OVER?

_____

_____

_____

_____

_____

_____

_____

_____

_____

_____

DATE: ___ /___/20___

PUT ON WOOL SOCKS, GET COZY UNDER A BLANKET, AND THINK ABOUT YOUR DAY.

WRITE DOWN ONE THING THAT MADE YOU SMILE TO YOURSELF AT YOUR DESK.

_____

_____

_____

_____

_____

_____

Spend 10 minutes reading Roxane Gay.

WRITE THE 3 THINGS YOU FEEL IMMEDIATELY AFTER.

Listen to the band the xx for 3 songs.

WRITE ABOUT THE AMBIENT WEIRDNESS.

_____

_____

_____

_____

_____

_____

_____

_____

_____

_____

WRITE DOWN 3 THINGS YOU COULD OFFER TO DO FOR A FRIEND THAT WOULD REALLY HELP THEM.

DOG SITTING? TEACHING THEM TO MAKE A NEW DISH? LENDING THEM A BOOK? TOMORROW, EMAIL THEM WITH THE SUGGESTION.

_____

_____

_____

_____

_____

_____

_____

DATE: __ /__/20__

Bring this journal into the bathroom and look at yourself in the mirror.

WRITE DOWN YOUR FAVORITE DETAIL.

_____

_____

_____

_____

_____

_____

_____

_____

_____

_____

DATE: ___/___/20___

Take this journal with you to your favorite spot for a chai tea, hot cider, or glass of wine. Sit with this page open and people-watch.

WHO CATCHES YOUR EYE? WHAT ARE THEY WEARING?
HOW ARE THEY SITTING? WHAT ARE THEY READING?

_____

_____

_____

_____

_____

_____

_____

_____

_____

DATE: ___ /___/20___

G'MORNING!
CONSIDER YOUR
AMBITIONS FOR TODAY.
WHAT NEGATIVE OR
BLOCKING THOUGHTS
CAN YOU PUSH AWAY?

AND WHAT AMBITIONS CAN YOU WELCOME IN? AT WORK,
AT HOME, IN YOUR FRIENDSHIPS, IN YOUR HEART. THINK IT
OVER.

_____

_____

_____

_____

_____

"**Nobody will stop you from creating. Do it tonight. Do it tomorrow. That is the way to make your soul grow... Before you go to bed, write a four-line poem. Make it as good as you can. Don't show it to anybody. Put it where nobody will find it.**"

⚡ KURT VONNEGUT

WRITE YOUR OWN 4-LINE POEM TONIGHT.

_____

_____

_____

_____

DATE: ___/___/20___

THIS PAGE IS RESERVED FOR A WINTRY WEEKEND TRIP, WHEN YOU'RE UNDER FLANNEL SHEETS SOMEWHERE.

WRITE DOWN 3 THINGS YOU'RE GRATEFUL FOR.

_____

_____

_____

_____

_____

_____

_____

_____

DATE: __ / __/20__

SPEND 20 MINUTES YOUTUBING EARLY '90S R&B.

WRITE DOWN THE 3 BEST OUTFITS YOU SEE.

_____

_____

_____

_____

_____

_____

_____

_____

_____

DATE: ___/___/20___

YOU'RE PRESIDENT FOR A DAY.

WHICH GROUPS DO YOU ADVOCATE FOR?

_____

_____

_____

_____

_____

_____

_____

_____

_____

Take yourself on a field trip to visit a tree.

AS YOU TAKE IN THE WINTER BRANCHES, WRITE DOWN 3 THINGS THE CHANGE IN SCENERY MAKES YOU FEEL.

_____

_____

_____

_____

_____

_____

_____

_____

_____

DATE: ___/___/20___

THINK ABOUT ONE TOPIC IN THE NEWS THAT YOU'VE NEVER QUITE UNDERSTOOD.

WRITE DOWN THE 3 ARTICLES YOU READ TO LEARN MORE ON THE TOPIC.

_____

_____

_____

_____

_____

_____

_____

_____

_____

DATE: ___ / ___ / 20___

 Power down, boo.

Turn off your phone,
your computer, your iPad,
you name it.

**SPEND 2 HOURS WITH NO ELECTRONICS AND WRITE
DOWN HOW YOU FEEL.**

_____

_____

_____

_____

_____

_____

DATE: __/__/20__

Listen to Frank Sinatra with a martini, in a housecoat. Waltz around, sing loudly.

WRITE DOWN YOUR FAVORITE LINE.

_____

_____

_____

_____

_____

_____

HAVE A GLASS OF WINE IN THE BATH. HAVE TWO.

WRITE DOWN YOUR FANTASY—THE THING THAT YOUR MIND DRIFTS TO.

_____

_____

_____

_____

_____

_____

_____

_____

DATE: ___ / ___ /20___

GO TO THE
MOVIES
BY YOURSELF.

RIGHT BEFORE THE MOVIE STARTS, WRITE DOWN WHAT
YOU'RE LOVING MOST ABOUT THE EXPERIENCE.

_____

_____

_____

_____

_____

_____

Write down the three authors you've always wanted to know more about.

_____

_____

_____

🔍 GOOGLE THEM RIGHT NOW.

_____

_____

_____

_____

_____

_____

_____

_____

"I WRITE ENTIRELY TO FIND OUT WHAT I'M THINKING, WHAT I'M LOOKING AT, WHAT I SEE AND WHAT IT MEANS. WHAT I WANT AND WHAT I FEAR."

⚡ JOAN DIDION

WHAT ARE YOU THINKING RIGHT NOW? WRITE IT DOWN
AND GIVE YOURSELF PERMISSION TO BE OKAY WITH IT,
HOWEVER SILLY, BEAUTIFUL, OR SCARY IT IS.

_____

_____

_____

_____

_____

DATE: ___/___/20___

THINK ABOUT
THAT ONE PERSON
YOU ALWAYS RUN INTO
IN THE OFFICE KITCHEN.

WRITE DOWN:
ONE THING YOU'RE CURIOUS ABOUT

_____

_____

ONE THING YOU IMAGINE
THEY READ EACH MORNING

_____

_____

ONE VACATION SPOT YOU IMAGINE
THEM TRAVELING TO THIS WINTER.

_____

_____

DATE: __/__/20__

YOU'RE WRITING THE SCREENPLAY OF YOUR LIFE. DESCRIBE THE OPENING CREDITS.

WHAT SONG IS PLAYING IN THE BACKGROUND? WHAT IS THE STYLE OF THE VISUALS? WHAT IMAGES DO WE SEE?

_____

_____

_____

_____

_____

_____

_____

DATE: __ / __ /20__

YOU SPEND THE DAY WITH HILLARY CLINTON.

WHAT DOES SHE TELL YOU?

_____

_____

_____

_____

_____

_____

_____

_____

_____

_____

★★★

YOU SPEND THE DAY WITH ★ MICHELLE ★ OBAMA.

WHAT DOES SHE TELL YOU?

_____

_____

_____

_____

_____

_____

_____

DATE: ___/___/20___

YOU SPEND THE DAY LIVING INSIDE A GARRY WINOGRAND PHOTO.

WRITE DOWN YOUR FAVORITE AND LEAST FAVORITE THINGS ABOUT THE NEW YORK CITY LANDSCAPE.

_____

_____

_____

_____

_____

_____

_____

_____

_____

_____

_____

Write down your top 10 favorite Instagram accounts.

WHAT DO YOU LOVE ABOUT THEM? TRY TO BE
AS PRECISE AS POSSIBLE.

1. _____

2. _____

3. _____

4. _____

5. _____

6. _____

7. _____

8. _____

9. _____

10. _____

DATE: ___ /___/20___

Write down one thing you can do every day to make your life a little better. Not earth-shattering, not overwhelming, but bite-size and achievable— like eating breakfast before you leave in the morning.

TOMORROW, GIVE IT A SHOT.

_____

_____

_____

_____

_____

_____

_____

_____

DATE: ___/___/20___

What was the last present you received in the mail?

WHO WAS IT FROM? WHAT IS THE BACKSTORY OF YOUR RELATIONSHIP? DID YOU LIKE THE GIFT?

_____

_____

_____

_____

_____

_____

_____

_____

_____

DATE: ___ / ___ /20___

Spend 15 minutes googling "meditation in America."

WHAT DO YOU DISCOVER?

_____

_____

_____

_____

_____

_____

_____

_____

_____

_____

_____

_____

DATE: ___/___/20___

Spend 15 minutes googling

Q "1960s sculpture in America."

WHAT DO YOU DISCOVER?

_____

_____

_____

_____

_____

_____

_____

_____

_____

_____

_____

DATE: __/__/20__

SPEND 15 MINUTES GOOGLING YOUR NAME.

WHAT DO YOU DISCOVER?

_____

_____

_____

_____

_____

_____

_____

_____

DATE: ___/___/20___

You know how Rick Astley's voice doesn't at all match his physical appearance?

WHAT QUALITY DO PEOPLE NOT EXPECT YOU TO HAVE?
HOW DOES IT SURPRISE PEOPLE?

_____

_____

_____

_____

_____

_____

_____

_____

_____

_____

_____

DATE: ___/___/20___

WRITE DOWN
THE HOBBIES YOU'VE
SPENT THE MOST
TIME CULTIVATING.

WRITE DOWN 3 NEW ONES YOU'D LIKE TO PICK UP.

_____

_____

_____

_____

_____

_____

_____

_____

_____

Which leader do you most admire and why?

_____

_____

_____

_____

_____

_____

_____

_____

DATE: ___ /___/20___

Write down the ice cream flavors that most match the personalities of the following individuals:

KATE MIDDLETON, OSCAR WILDE, PENÉLOPE CRUZ, AND YOUR 4TH GRADE TEACHER.

DATE: ___ /___/20___

DESCRIBE THE LAST TIME YOU WERE IN THE WOODS.

THE AIR, THE SCENTS, THE BRIGHTNESS OF THE SUN, THE CONVERSATION.

_____

_____

_____

_____

_____

_____

_____

_____

_____

_____

"JUST SPEAK VERY LOUDLY AND QUICKLY, AND STATE YOUR POSITION WITH UTTER CONVICTION, AS THE FRENCH DO, AND YOU'LL HAVE A MARVELOUS TIME!"

⚡ JULIA CHILD

WRITE DOWN A MOTTO YOU BELIEVE IN, THAT YOU'VE CREATED.

_____

_____

_____

_____

Think of a loss you've experienced, big or small. It could be your ice cream falling to the sidewalk or your lover walking out the door. What's the first thing that comes to mind?

_____

_____

_____

_____

_____

_____

DATE: __ / __ /20__

IMAGINE YOUR LIFE AS A NEW YORKER COVER.

DESCRIBE THE IMAGE AND THE STYLE OF THE ILLUSTRATION.

_____

_____

_____

_____

_____

_____

_____

_____

_____

DATE: ___/___/20___

TODAY, YOU'RE
A FISHERMAN LIVING
IN RURAL MAINE.

THE SNOW IS FALLING OUTSIDE THE WINDOWS OF YOUR
BIRCH CABIN, THE LOGS ARE CRACKLING IN THE FIREPLACE.
DESCRIBE THE 3 PAINTINGS ON YOUR WALL.

_____

_____

_____

_____

_____

_____

_____

_____

_____

_____

_____

_____

WHAT POLITICAL ISSUE DO YOU FEEL MOST PASSIONATE ABOUT AND WHY?

DATE: ___ /___/20___

"i am not a hotel room/
i am home / i am not the
whiskey you want /
i am the water you need /
don't come here with
expectations / and try to make
a vacation out of me."

FROM *MILK AND HONEY* ⚡ BY RUPI KAUR

WHO HAS TRIED TO MAKE A VACATION OUT OF YOU AND
WHAT DID YOU DO ABOUT IT?

_____

_____

_____

_____

_____

YOU'RE A REPORTER AND YOU SPEND A MONTH WITH ONE BAND.

WHO IS IT AND WHAT DO YOU LEARN? ON THE ROAD, IN THEIR HOTEL ROOMS, DURING SOUND CHECKS, AND EATING LATE-NIGHT CHEESEBURGERS AT THE DINER TOGETHER.

_____

_____

_____

_____

_____

_____

_____

_____

_____

_____

_____

You part the velvet curtains and find yourself in the back room of a Russian teahouse.

WHAT HAPPENS NEXT?

_____

_____

_____

_____

_____

_____

_____

_____

DATE: ___ /___/20___

DESCRIBE YOUR HAIR A YEAR AGO.

DESCRIBE YOUR HAIR NOW.

_____

_____

_____

_____

_____

_____

_____

_____

_____

_____

_____

_____

You wake up and find yourself in yellow silk sheets, croissants, berries, and coffee to your right. Someone opens the door.

WHO IS IT? WHAT DO THEY TELL YOU?

_____

_____

_____

_____

_____

_____

_____

_____

_____

_____

_____

_____

What is the best advice you've ever received from an elderly person?

WHO WAS IT?

_____

_____

_____

_____

_____

_____

_____

_____

_____

_____

_____

_____

_____

DATE: ___/___/20___

Flannel or cotton?

WHY?

_____

_____

_____

_____

_____

_____

_____

_____

_____

_____

_____

DATE: ___/___/20___

Winter can be a lonely season.

DESCRIBE THE LAST TIME YOU REALLY SAT WITH YOUR THOUGHTS, FLOATING IN THE FEELINGS.

_____

_____

_____

_____

_____

_____

_____

_____

_____

_____

DATE: __ /__/20__

YOU HAVE
$3,000
TO SPEND—

AND THAT MONEY HAS TO BE SPENT ON ONE DECADENT
WINTER ACCESSORY. WHAT IS IT? PLEASE DESCRIBE.

DATE: ___/___/20___

YOU SPEND 3 MONTHS OF THE WINTER IN A REMOTE VILLAGE IN ALASKA AND YOU'RE ALLOWED ONE BOOK, ONE FRIEND, AND ONE BOTTLE OF WINE.

TELL ME ABOUT ALL 3.

_____

_____

_____

_____

_____

DATE: __/__/20__

Describe your stream of consciousness from last weekend, cuddled in your sheets.

WHAT WERE YOU THINKING ABOUT? INCLUDE THE GOOD, THE BAD, AND THE UGLY.

_____

_____

_____

_____

_____

_____

_____

_____

_____

"Sometimes you have to play a long time to be able to play like yourself."

⚡ MILES DAVIS

WHAT HAVE YOU BEEN WORKING AT STEADILY?
IT COULD EVEN BE BEING YOURSELF.

_____

_____

_____

_____

_____

_____

_____

EVERY NEIGHBORHOOD HAS ONE ICON, ONE FAMOUS (OR INFAMOUS) CHARACTER.

DESCRIBE THIS LOCAL CELEBRITY (EXAMPLE: THE OLD LADY NEXT DOOR WHO IS ALWAYS IN A YANKEES JERSEY, CHAIN-SMOKING, TEXTING ON A FLIP PHONE).

_____

_____

_____

_____

_____

_____

_____

Spend 5 minutes googling "winter spice."

WRITE DOWN WHAT YOU LEARN.

_____

_____

_____

_____

_____

_____

_____

_____

_____

Justin Vernon, from Bon Iver, spent an entire winter recording an album in a cabin in Wisconsin.

WHAT WOULD YOU LIKE TO SPEND THE ENTIRE SEASON
DOING, UNINTERRUPTED?

_____

_____

_____

_____

_____

_____

_____

_____

_____

_____

_____

_____

DATE: ___/___/20___

HOW DID YOU FEEL THE LAST TIME YOU PASSED A HOMELESS PERSON?

Write down everything that happened on your street the last time it snowed.

_____

_____

_____

_____

_____

_____

_____

_____

DATE: ___/___/20___

If you were to put on your favorite fisherman sweater, lace up your winter boots, and truck through the woods to a fortune teller, what topics would you want to hear about?

AND WHAT OMENS DO YOU THINK YOU'D RECEIVE?

_____

_____

_____

_____

_____

_____

_____

DATE: ___/___/20___

"Little darling, it's been a long cold lonely winter."

"HERE COMES THE SUN" ⚡ THE BEATLES

HOW HAS THIS WINTER BEEN FOR YOU? WHAT WOULD YOUR MEMOIR OF THIS WINTER BE TITLED?

_____

_____

_____

_____

_____

_____

_____

IF YOU COULD SPEND A MONTH TRAVELING ON A BOAT AROUND NEW ZEALAND AND AUSTRALIA, WHAT WOULD YOUR ADVENTURE ENTAIL?

DESCRIBE YOUR ROOM, SITTING ON THE DECK OF THE SHIP, YOUR WEIRD DINNER COMPANIONS.

_____

_____

_____

_____

_____

_____

_____

_____

_____

DATE: __/__/20__

YOU WAKE UP IN 1963 IN LONDON. IT'S WINTER HERE TOO.

WHAT'S THE THING YOU MISS MOST ABOUT YOUR OLD LIFE?

_____

_____

_____

_____

_____

_____

_____

_____

DATE: ___/___/20___

YOU'RE INVITED FOR TEA WITH THE QUEEN OF ENGLAND.

YOU'RE ESCORTED DOWN THE MARBLE STAIRCASE INTO HER CHAMBER, WHERE THE FIRE IS BLAZING. YOU HAVE 5 MINUTES TO TELL HER A TRUE STORY TO MAKE HER LAUGH—WHAT IS IT?

_____

_____

_____

_____

_____

_____

_____

DATE: __ /__ /20__

With your eyes closed, spend 2 minutes imagining hiking through icy wilderness. Could be Alaska, could be Mt. Everest.

YOU'VE BEEN SLEEPING IN A TENT FOR 6 WEEKS, SOLO. WHAT FEARS OR ANXIETIES DOES THIS PROVOKE?

_____

_____

_____

_____

_____

_____

_____

_____

_____

YOU OPEN THE DOOR AND FIND AMY SCHUMER STANDING THERE.

"DO YOU HAVE AN EXTRA CINNAMON STICK?"
SHE ASKS. "I NEED IT FOR MY HOT CIDER."

DESCRIBE THE SCENE FROM THERE.

_____

_____

_____

_____

_____

_____

_____

_____

_____

DATE: ___/___/20___

THINK ABOUT ALL THE DECEMBERS OF YOUR LIFE.

WHICH HAS BEEN THE MOST DRAMATIC AND WHY?

_____

_____

_____

_____

_____

_____

_____

_____

_____

_____

_____

_____

DATE: ___/___/20___

You're invited to participate in a special government experiment where you will be able to travel back in time to 1812 through an induced coma.

YOU WILL BE PAID $5 MILLION AND WILL BE "ASLEEP" FOR 3 MONTHS. WHAT WOULD STOP YOU FROM DOING IT?

_____

_____

_____

_____

_____

_____

_____

THE CLOCK STRIKES MIDNIGHT ON THE LEFT BANK IN PARIS, YOU'RE THERE WITH CHAMPAGNE AND SPARKLERS.

WHAT DO YOU WISH FOR?

_____

_____

_____

_____

_____

_____

DATE: __/__/20__

YOU GET A PHONE CALL FROM BERLIN.

A MYSTERIOUS BENEFACTOR IS DONATING THEIR VINEYARD TO YOU—AND IT'S IN TUSCANY. WHAT ARE YOUR NEXT STEPS? TO ABANDON YOUR CURRENT LIFE AND FLY AWAY, TO RESELL? AND WHAT DOES THIS SAY ABOUT YOUR CURRENT MOOD?

_____

_____

_____

_____

_____

_____

_____

_____

DATE: ___ /___ /20___

YOUR HOT-AIR BALLOON SPUTTERS, AND SUDDENLY YOU'RE FALLING, FALLING, FALLING, INTO DEEP, DARK WOODS.
YOU HIT THE GROUND, BARELY SURVIVING.

WHO'S THE FIRST PERSON THAT COMES TO MIND? IS IT SOMEONE YOU WOULD CONTACT? WHY OR WHY NOT?

_____

_____

_____

_____

_____

_____

_____

DATE: __/__/20__

Close your eyes and focus on the image of gloves. Are they uneven and woolly, or long and satin?

WHO IN YOUR LIFE EMBODIES THIS ARTICLE OF CLOTHING? AND HOW DO/DID THEY WEAR THEM?

_____

_____

_____

_____

_____

_____

_____

_____

What are you most nostalgic for from the winters of your childhood?

_____

_____

_____

_____

_____

_____

_____

_____

_____

DATE: ___ /___/20___

YOU ARE HAVING A HOT CHOCOLATE BY THE FIRE WITH JAMES CORDEN.

YOU END UP SINGING AN INCREDIBLE DUET MEDLEY OF YOUR FAVORITE HOLIDAY TUNES. WHAT ARE THEY AND IN WHAT ORDER?

_____

_____

_____

_____

_____

_____

_____

_____

_____

_____

DATE: ___/___/20___

IF SOMEONE YOU DIDN'T KNOW SHOWED UP AT YOUR FRONT DOOR ASKING FOR SHELTER, WHAT WOULD YOU DO?

YOU'RE REINCARNATED AS A SNOWFLAKE.

WHAT DO YOU SEE AS YOU'RE SWEPT THROUGH THE AIR AND WHERE DO YOU LAND?

DATE: ___ /___ /20___

WHAT CHANGE ARE YOU WAITING FOR— WINTER TO SPRING?

TO HEART? TO SOUL?

_____

_____

_____

_____

_____

_____

_____

_____

_____

_____

_____

_____

_____

DATE: __ /__/20__

Imagine yourself hanging off an enormous mountain, ice picks dug into the cliff face.

YOU LOOK TO THE GROUND, ASTONISHED, 15,000 FEET IN THE AIR. WHO WOULD BE MOST IMPACTED IF YOU FELL?

_____

_____

_____

_____

_____

_____

_____

_____

_____

_____

_____

_____

DATE: ___ / ___ /20___

READ "THE LOVE SONG OF J. ALFRED PRUFROCK."

WRITE DOWN THE PARTS THAT RESONATE WITH YOU AND WHAT THEY CONJURE UP.

_____

_____

_____

_____

_____

_____

_____

_____

_____

_____

DATE: __/__/20__

ACCORDING TO THE MUSICAL *RENT* THERE ARE "SEASONS OF LOVE."

THERE ARE ALSO SEASONS OF HURT, HELPFULNESS, POISON, AND BOUNTY—OR WHATEVER YOU DECIDE THERE ARE. WHAT SEASON OF YOUR LIFE ARE YOU IN?

_____

_____

_____

_____

_____

_____

_____

_____

_____

DATE: ___ /___ /20___

IMAGINE A FIELD OF LAVENDER—THE FLOWERS GROWING TOWARD THE SKY, THE PURPLE SEEMINGLY ENDLESS.

THERE'S SOMEONE WAITING FOR YOU AT THE END OF THAT FIELD WITH AN IMPORTANT MESSAGE. IT'S A MESSAGE FROM YOUR PAST THAT WILL MAKE YOU FEEL REALLY GOOD. WHAT COULD IT BE?

_____

_____

_____

_____

_____

_____

What animal feels like winter to you?

_____

_____

_____

_____

_____

_____

_____

_____

_____

_____

DATE: ___ / ___ /20___

THE APOCALYPSE COMES AND YOUR HOME IS COVERED IN SNOW, UNLEAVABLE, FOR DAYS.

WHO DO YOU WANT THERE WITH YOU—FOR EVERY BREAKFAST, EVERY BOOK, EVERY SONG, EVERY MINUTE?

_____

_____

_____

_____

_____

_____

_____

_____

_____

The snow this year is made of cotton and silk, sugar and lace.

DESCRIBE HOW IT LOOKS COVERING THE FIELDS CLOSEST TO YOU.

_____

_____

_____

_____

_____

_____

_____

_____

_____

WHICH VOICE IN YOUR LIFE MOST REMINDS YOU OF WINTER?

DATE: ___ /___/20___

ANDY WARHOL COMES OVER FOR TEA. HE WANTS TO TELL YOU ABOUT THE BEST WINTER OF HIS LIFE, IN 1979.

IF YOU COULD GO BACK TO THE PRE–CELL PHONES, PRE-INTERNET FACTORY, WHAT WOULD YOU DO DIFFERENTLY?

_____
_____
_____
_____
_____
_____
_____
_____
_____

DATE: ___/___/20___

"SO AS I'M STANDING AT THE STATION / IT MIGHT BE OVER SOON / (ALL THESE YEARS)."

"22 OVER S∞∞N" ⚡ BON IVER

WHAT DO "THESE YEARS" SIGNIFY FOR YOU? IF THESE
YEARS ARE ALMOST OVER, WHAT'S THE ONE THING WE
SHOULD KNOW?

_____

_____

_____

_____

_____

_____

AN XMAS COOKIE IS NAMED AFTER YOU.

WHAT IS IT CALLED AND WHAT DOES IT TASTE LIKE?

_____

_____

_____

_____

_____

_____

_____

_____

_____

_____

DATE: ___ / ___ /20___

"To err is human, forgive divine."

WHAT DOES THAT MEAN TO YOU? AND DO YOU BELIEVE IT?

_____

_____

_____

_____

_____

_____

_____

_____

_____

_____

_____

_____

_____

_____

WHAT'S SOMETHING YOU DO EVERY DAY THAT SOMEONE ELSE TAUGHT YOU HOW TO DO?

WHAT WAS IT AND WHO WERE THEY?

_____

_____

_____

_____

_____

_____

_____

_____

_____

_____

_____

What single thing is most necessary for you to feel snug?

IT'S ALMOST SPRING. WHAT ARE YOU GOING TO DO?

DATE: ___ / ___ / 20___

Pour yourself a fat glass of wine and put your feet up on your couch.

WRITE DOWN ONE THING THAT HAPPENED THIS WEEK THAT LEFT YOU FEELING RATTLED.

_____

_____

_____

_____

_____

_____

_____

_____

DATE: ___/___/20___

WRITE DOWN THE NAME OF ONE WOMAN IN YOUR FAMILY WHO INSPIRES YOU AND WHY YOU ADMIRE HER.

WHILE YOU'RE AT IT, GRAB A PIECE OF YOUR FAVORITE STATIONERY AND SEND HER A LETTER ABOUT IT AS WELL.

_____

_____

_____

_____

_____

_____

_____

_____

DATE: __ / __ /20 __

WALK DOWN THE STREET TO YOUR FAVORITE FLOWER SHOP AND ADMIRE THE BLOOMS.

WHAT MEMORY DO THOSE FLOWERS CONJURE FOR YOU?

_____

_____

_____

_____

_____

_____

_____

DATE: ___/___/20___

PUT ON "END OF TIME" BY BEYONCÉ, CLOSE YOUR EYES, AND LISTEN TO THAT KILLER BEAT.

WHAT IMAGE COMES TO MIND? WHERE DO YOU WANT TO BE RIGHT NOW?

_____

_____

_____

_____

_____

_____

_____

_____

_____

_____

_____

_____

_____

DATE: __/__/20__

Write down 10 people you've met but would like to know better.

EMAIL THEM TOMORROW ABOUT A DINNER PARTY AT YOUR SPOT.

_____

_____

_____

_____

_____

_____

_____

_____

_____

_____

DATE: ___/___/20___

"The more clearly we can focus our attention on the wonders and realities of the universe about us, the less taste we shall have for destruction."

⚡ RACHEL CARSON

WRITE DOWN 3 THINGS ABOUT YOURSELF THAT ARE
WONDERFUL, AND WRITE DOWN 3 THINGS THAT YOU
ADMIRE IN OTHERS.

_____

_____

_____

_____

_____

_____

_____

DATE: ___/___/20___

"EVERYBODY THINKS THEY HAVE GOOD TASTE AND A SENSE OF HUMOR, BUT THEY COULDN'T POSSIBLY ALL HAVE GOOD TASTE."

⚡ MARIE IN *WHEN HARRY MET SALLY*

NAME ONE THING THAT YOU ASPIRE TO HAVE BUT DON'T:
A GREAT PALATE, A GOOD EYE, A WAY WITH CHOPSTICKS.
AND THEN WRITE DOWN 3 THINGS YOU COULD DO
TO IMPROVE.

_____

_____

_____

_____

_____

_____

WHAT ARE THE FREELANCE PROJECTS, SIDE GIGS, OR LITTLE THINGS YOU CAN DO TO MAKE A NEST EGG OF CASH MONEEEY?

MAKE IT REAL BY FILLING A JAR LABELED **"CASH MONEY"** WITH SCRAPS OF PAPER AND ASK EVERYONE WHO COMES OVER TO LEAVE AN IDEA. FROM HERE ON OUT, YOU'RE HUSTLING.

_____

_____

_____

_____

_____

_____

_____

DATE: ___/___/20___

"A lot of people...have a problem being true to their self. They have a problem looking into the mirror and looking directly into their own soul... I can look directly into my face and find my soul."

⚡ TUPAC

WRITE DOWN 3 THINGS YOU'RE PROUD OF YOURSELF FOR.

_____

_____

_____

_____

_____

_____

Tomorrow, build in time for a cup of coffee in a local park near your office.

TAKE THIS JOURNAL AND WRITE 3 THINGS YOU SEE SITTING THERE: THE COLOR OF THOSE BODACIOUS TULIPS, THE DOGS STROLLING BY, THE ANXIETY YOU FEEL.

_____

_____

_____

_____

_____

_____

_____

_____

_____

_____

DATE: ___/___/20___

"SOME OF US ARE BORN REBELLIOUS."

⚡ PATTI SMITH

HOW WERE YOU BORN?

_____

_____

_____

_____

_____

_____

_____

_____

_____

_____

_____

_____

_____

"BE A LONER. THAT GIVES YOU TIME TO WONDER..."

⚡ ALBERT EINSTEIN

GO FOR A WALK. WRITE DOWN WHAT YOU SEE AND HOW THE AIR FEELS.

_____

_____

_____

_____

_____

_____

_____

DATE: ___/___/20___

"IT TOOK ME A LIFETIME."

⚡ PABLO PICASSO

WHAT IS THE THING YOU'RE WILLING TO SPEND A LIFETIME DOING?

_____

_____

_____

_____

_____

_____

_____

_____

_____

DATE: ___/___/20___

"Try to learn to breathe deeply, really to taste food when you eat, and when you sleep, really to sleep. Try as much as possible to be wholly alive... You will be dead soon enough."

⚡ WILLIAM SAROYAN

WHAT WILL YOU DO TOMORROW TO BE MORE WHOLLY ALIVE?

_____

_____

_____

_____

_____

_____

DATE: ___/___/20___

"TO MAKE LIVING ITSELF AN ART, THAT IS THE GOAL."

⚡ HENRY MILLER

AGREE OR DISAGREE? IF YES, WHY? IF NO, WHY?

_____

_____

_____

_____

_____

_____

_____

_____

_____

_____

WHAT HAS BEEN ON YOUR MIND THAT YOU HAVEN'T FELT YOU COULD CONFESS?

WRITE IT HERE, THEN CALL YOUR FRIEND, THE ONE WHO LOVES COFFEE, AND TELL THEM OVER A CUP.

_____

_____

_____

_____

_____

_____

_____

_____

_____

_____

DATE: ___/___/20___

TODAY, YOU LIVE IN A PINK HOUSE IN THE SUBURBS. YOUR YARD HAS SUNFLOWERS AND TOPIARY FROM THE '70S.

WHAT IS YOUR FAVORITE THING ABOUT THIS MAKE-BELIEVE LIFE?

_____

_____

_____

_____

_____

TODAY, YOU LIVE IN A BROWNSTONE THAT WAS BUILT IN THE 1800S, AND YOU HAVE A LEOPARD-PRINT CHAISE LONGUE IN YOUR DRESSING ROOM.

WHAT IS YOUR FAVORITE THING ABOUT THIS MAKE-BELIEVE LIFE?

_____

_____

_____

_____

_____

_____

_____

_____

DATE: ___ / ___ /20___

WRITE DOWN ONE THING YOU'RE ASHAMED OF.

NO JUDGMENT.

_____

_____

_____

_____

_____

_____

_____

_____

_____

_____

_____

_____

_____

DATE: ___/___/20___

Listen to "Something to Talk About," performed by Bonnie Raitt, and scrub your entire home, top to bottom.

DESCRIBE YOUR HANDS AFTER THE FACT—THEIR TEMPERATURE, THEIR TEXTURE, THE VIBRATIONS.

_____

_____

_____

_____

_____

DATE: __/__/20__

Arrange your lipstick by color, darkest to lightest.

PICK ONE AT RANDOM AND WRITE ABOUT THE FIRST
CELEBRITY THE COLOR BRINGS TO MIND, AND HOW YOU
WANT TO CHANNEL THEM THIS SPRING.

_____

_____

_____

_____

_____

_____

_____

_____

_____

DATE: ___/___/20___

"YOU HAVE TO ACT AS IF IT WERE POSSIBLE TO RADICALLY TRANSFORM THE WORLD. AND YOU HAVE TO DO IT ALL THE TIME."

⚡ ANGELA DAVIS

THINK ABOUT ONE SMALL WAY YOU CAN CHANGE YOUR OWN WORLD. WHAT IS THAT THING?

_____

_____

_____

_____

_____

WHAT IS YOUR SINGLE GREATEST FEAR?

_____

_____

_____

_____

_____

_____

_____

_____

_____

_____

_____

_____

_____

_____

WHAT IS YOUR SINGLE GREATEST TRIUMPH?

_____

_____

_____

_____

_____

_____

_____

_____

_____

_____

THERE ARE DREAMERS, THERE ARE DOERS.

THERE ARE PEOPLE WHO ARE BOTH. WHERE DO YOU FIT?
AND HOW DO YOU FEEL ABOUT IT?

_____

_____

_____

_____

_____

_____

_____

_____

ON APRIL 21, 2016, PRINCE DIED, AND THE RAIN WAS PURPLE.

WHERE WERE YOU? WHAT WERE YOU DOING? DESCRIBE THAT AFTERNOON.

_____

_____

_____

_____

_____

_____

_____

_____

DATE: ___ /___ /20___

THINK OF YOUR FUTURE SON, DAUGHTER, GRANDCHILD.

WRITE DOWN THE FIRST IMAGE THAT COMES TO MIND WHEN YOU IMAGINE YOURSELF AT THAT TIME. ARE YOU CHANGING A DIAPER? APPLE PICKING? PAINTING IN A STUDIO?

_____

_____

_____

_____

_____

_____

_____

_____

_____

THE BEST NAIL POLISH COLORS HAVE THE BEST NAMES: GOTTA LOVE "HAPPY WIFE HAPPY LIFE" RED.

WRITE DOWN 5 POTENTIAL NAIL POLISH NAMES
THAT ARE EQUALLY AS RIDICULOUS.

_____

_____

_____

_____

_____

_____

Imagine a beautiful but slightly dusty porcelain coffee cup. It's painted with pink roses that are faded and smudged with lipstick. And it's sitting on a matching saucer.

WHO WOULD YOU LIKE TO SHARE A CUP OF COFFEE WITH (CAN BE ANYONE—DEAD OR ALIVE, FAMOUS OR FAMILIAR)? WHAT WOULD YOU TALK ABOUT?

_____

_____

_____

_____

_____

DATE: ___ /___ /20___

IMAGINE YOU'RE A JOCKEY IN THE KENTUCKY DERBY.

YOU'RE BALANCED ON YOUR HORSE WHEN THE BELL GOES OFF. DESCRIBE THE FEELING OF RACING AROUND THE TRACK: THE OTHER HORSES, THE SPEED, THE COLORS, THE LIGHTS. WHAT GIVES YOU THIS KIND OF RUSH IN YOUR DAY-TO-DAY LIFE?

_____

_____

_____

_____

_____

_____

_____

_____

"it takes grace to remain kind in cruel situations."

FROM *MILK AND HONEY* ⚡ BY RUPI KAUR

DESCRIBE A SITUATION WHERE YOU REMAINED KIND IN
THE FACE OF CRUELTY.

_____

_____

_____

_____

_____

DATE: ___/___/20___

WHICH POLITICIAN DO YOU ADMIRE MOST AND WHY?

★★

DATE: ___/___/20___

TODAY, YOU'RE ONE-HALF OF A CELEBRITY COUPLE

(WITH A FAMOUS VERSION OF YOUR REAL PARTNER OR AN ACTUAL STAR). DESCRIBE YOUR RELATIONSHIP, AS SEEN THROUGH THE EYES OF THE PAPARAZZI.

_____

_____

_____

_____

_____

_____

_____

_____

_____

_____

_____

DATE: __/__/20__

EVERYONE HAS A SCAR, BIRTHMARK, OR ODDITY THAT THEY ARE EMBARRASSED ABOUT.

WHAT IS YOURS?

_____

_____

_____

_____

_____

_____

_____

_____

WHAT IF YOUR FAVORITE ARTISTS HAD DECIDED NOT TO GO FOR THEIR DREAMS?

(LIKE WHAT IF STEVIE WONDER HAD DECIDED TO JUST SING IN THE SHOWER AND LEAVE IT AT THAT?) WHO ARE THE 5 ARTISTS, CREATORS, OR DREAMERS YOU'D BE LOST WITHOUT?

_____

_____

_____

_____

_____

_____

_____

_____

_____

_____

"Vulnerability is the birthplace of everything we hold dear: human connection, creativity, new ideas—you have to risk everything in order to do something new."

⚡ NATE BERKUS

WHEN DID YOU LAST FEEL TRULY VULNERABLE
AND WHAT DID IT TEACH YOU?

_____

_____

_____

_____

_____

_____

_____

You're zooming down the Pacific Coast Highway in a Ferrari California Spider from 1959, valued at $9 million.

WHO ARE YOU ON YOUR WAY TO SEE?

_____

_____

_____

_____

_____

_____

_____

WHAT'S YOUR FAVORITE OUTFIT FROM THE CINEMATIC GEM *CLUELESS?*

_____

_____

_____

_____

_____

_____

_____

_____

_____

_____

DATE: __/__/20__

JOAN DIDION WROTE *THE YEAR OF MAGICAL THINKING.*

IN YOUR WORLD,
THIS IS THE YEAR OF_____THINKING.

ELABORATE.

_____

_____

_____

_____

_____

_____

_____

_____

_____

WHICH CHARACTER FROM HBO'S *SEX AND THE CITY* ARE YOU?

WHICH ONE DO YOUR FRIENDS SAY YOU ARE?

_____

_____

_____

_____

_____

_____

_____

_____

_____

_____

DATE: __ /__/20__

YOU SPEND A MONTH PAINTING WITH MONET IN FRANCE.

WHAT IN YOUR LIFE DO YOU CHOOSE TO IMMORTALIZE
WITH THE HELP OF A MASTER?

_____

_____

_____

_____

_____

_____

_____

_____

_____

DATE: __/__/20__

WHICH SAINT ARE YOU MOST INTRIGUED BY?

RELIGIOUS OR OTHERWISE...

_____

_____

_____

_____

_____

_____

_____

_____

_____

_____

_____

THINK ABOUT THE LAST TIME YOUR HEART ACHED.

WHY WAS IT SO HEAVY AND WHAT DID YOU DO TO RECOVER?

_____

_____

_____

_____

_____

_____

_____

_____

_____

_____

DATE: ___/___/20___

WHAT ALBUM SIGNIFIES SPRING FOR YOU?

WRITE DOWN YOUR FAVORITE TRACKS AND YOUR
FAVORITE RELATED MEMORIES.

_____

_____

_____

_____

_____

_____

_____

_____

_____

You're given an Airbnb stay, free of charge.

WHERE WOULD IT BE? WHAT KIND OF ACCOMMODATION IS IT? WHO WOULD YOU BRING?

_____

_____

_____

_____

_____

_____

_____

_____

_____

WRITE DOWN 10 REASONS YOU HATE, LOVE, OR FEEL INDIFFERENT ABOUT PATTI SMITH.

1. _____
2. _____
3. _____
4. _____
5. _____
6. _____
7. _____
8. _____
9. _____
10. _____

Write down 10 reasons you hate, love, or feel indifferent about Tim Burton.

1. _____
2. _____
3. _____
4. _____
5. _____
6. _____
7. _____
8. _____
9. _____
10. _____

TOMORROW YOU WAKE UP ON A RIVER-BOAT IN THAILAND.

WITH YOU ARE 3 ITEMS YOU CHOSE TO BRING FROM YOUR PREVIOUS LIFE. WHAT ARE THEY?

WHAT THOUGHTS KEEP YOU AWAKE AT NIGHT? AND ARE THEY ABOUT THINGS YOU CAN SOLVE?

WRITE DOWN A FEW STEPS OR POSITIVE THOUGHTS THAT MIGHT HELP COUNTER THEM.

_____

_____

_____

_____

_____

_____

_____

_____

_____

_____

"I have to constantly reidentify myself to myself, reactivate my own standards, my own convictions about what I'm doing and why."

⚡ **NINA SIMONE**

IF YOU STOP FOR 2 MINUTES AND THINK ABOUT "REIDENTIFYING" YOURSELF, WHAT COMES TO MIND? WHAT QUALITIES HAVE YOU IDENTIFIED IN YOURSELF THAT ARE NEW?

_____

_____

_____

_____

_____

DATE: ___/___/20___

YOU'RE GIVEN THE SKELETON KEY TO ONE ENORMOUSLY FAMOUS ARCHIVE.

WHAT DOES IT CONTAIN?

_____

_____

_____

_____

_____

_____

_____

_____

_____

_____

Imagine walking through a grove of cherry blossoms and taking shelter under the biggest one as the first spring rain pours down.

WHAT THOUGHTS ARE GOING THROUGH YOUR MIND?

_____

_____

_____

_____

_____

DATE: ___/___/20___

WHAT IS YOUR SINGLE GREATEST FEAR AT THIS MOMENT?

TERRORISM, YOUR PARENTS GETTING SICK, A RELATIONSHIP
ENDING? DESCRIBE IT—AND TRY TO LET YOURSELF FALL
INTO THE BLACKNESS OF THE THOUGHTS TO GET FAMILIAR
WITH THEM. WRITE ABOUT THE PEOPLE WHO GIVE YOU THE
MOST COMFORT WHEN DARK THOUGHTS DESCEND.

_____

_____

_____

_____

_____

WHAT DOES THE WORD "FREEDOM" MEAN FOR YOU THIS SPRING?

IS IT NO FUCKS TO GIVE AND WEARING WHATEVER YOU WANT AND READING WHATEVER YOU WANT?

_____

_____

_____

_____

_____

_____

_____

_____

_____

_____

_____

DATE: __/__/20__

WRITE DOWN YOUR GREATEST SEXUAL FANTASY.

NO JUDGMENTS.

_____

_____

_____

_____

_____

_____

_____

_____

_____

_____

_____

DATE: ___ / ___ /20___

PRESIDENT OBAMA ASKS YOU TO ADDRESS THIS YEAR'S HARVARD GRADUATING CLASS.

WRITE DOWN THE FIRST 10 LINES OF YOUR SPEECH.

_____

_____

_____

_____

_____

_____

_____

_____

YOU GO ON A SAFARI WITH ERNEST HEMINGWAY.

AS YOU'RE DRINKING A NEGRONI, LEOPARDS AT YOUR FEET, HE TELLS YOU ABOUT HIS GREATEST ADVENTURE. WHAT STORY DO YOU OFFER IN RESPONSE?

_____

_____

_____

_____

_____

_____

_____

_____

DATE: ___/___/20___

The Hope Diamond arrives at your doorstep, tied with a bow.

WHAT ARE THE FIRST THOUGHTS THAT COME TO MIND? AND WHO IS YOUR FIRST PHONE CALL?

_____

_____

_____

_____

_____

_____

_____

_____

_____

DATE: ___/___/20___

THINK ABOUT THE LAST TIME YOU WERE REAAAAALLLY HOMESICK.

WHO WAS IT FOR?

_____

_____

_____

_____

_____

_____

_____

_____

What's your favorite time of day and what's perfect about it?

_____

_____

_____

_____

_____

_____

_____

_____

_____

_____

A motorcycle is sent to your office with a card that has a single line on it.

WHAT DOES IT SAY?

"A TOUCH OF MADNESS IS, I THINK, ALMOST ALWAYS NECESSARY FOR CONSTRUCTING A DESTINY."

⚡ MARGUERITE YOURCENAR

WHAT DO YOU THINK YOUR DESTINY IS?

_____

_____

_____

_____

_____

_____

_____

DATE: ___/___/20___

You're in Rome, awaiting your table at a Michelin-starred restaurant, when Mario Batali appears, asking if he can share your table.

WHAT DO YOU EAT?

_____

_____

_____

_____

_____

_____

_____

_____

_____

_____

You can be a dishwasher, a cobbler, or a vet.

WHAT DO YOU CHOOSE AND WHY?

_____

_____

_____

_____

_____

_____

_____

_____

_____

_____

_____

_____

DATE: ___ /___/20___

YOU WAKE UP AND YOUR LIFE IS A FILM NOIR.

WHAT STICKS OUT MOST ON YOUR WALK TO WORK IN BLACK AND WHITE?

_____

_____

_____

_____

_____

_____

_____

_____

_____

_____

_____

_____

DATE: __/__/20__

What's your favorite thing right now?

FLOWER, ALBUM, PERSON, FOOD, SMELL, ENVIRONMENT, SOUND—WHATEVER IT IS, WRITE ABOUT IT.

_____

_____

_____

_____

_____

_____

_____

_____

_____

_____

DATE: ___/___/20___

A MYSTERIOUS OLD LADY WITH A FAKE FLOWER IN HER HAIR AND CLOGS ON HER FEET TAKES YOU ON AN ADVENTURE— A RIVERBOAT, A MUSEUM, AND HER SPECIAL SPOT, WHICH YOU FIND EXTREMELY SURPRISING.

WHERE IS IT AND WHO WOULD YOU TAKE THERE?

_____

_____

_____

_____

_____

_____

_____

A BIG SPRING BREEZE WHIPS ON THROUGH, TAKING YOUR HOUSE INTO THE HEAVENS.

YOU LAND IN SWEDEN, AND PLOPPPPP RIGHT DOWN TO THE GROUND. WHAT ITEM IN YOUR HOUSE IS THE FIRST THING YOU CHECK TO SEE IF IT SURVIVED?

_____

_____

_____

_____

_____

_____

_____

_____

_____

TRY TO DESCRIBE WHAT A PIANO SOUNDS LIKE.

_____

_____

_____

_____

_____

_____

_____

_____

_____

_____

_____

_____

_____

DATE: ___/___/20___

IF YOU'RE REINCARNATED, WHAT OR WHO WOULD YOU LIKE TO COME BACK AS?

_____
_____
_____
_____
_____
_____
_____
_____
_____
_____
_____
_____
_____

Spend 10 minutes googling

Q global warming

WHAT DO YOU LEARN AND HOW CAN YOU CHANGE YOUR HABITS ACCORDINGLY?

_____

_____

_____

_____

_____

_____

_____

_____

_____

_____

_____

WHAT ARE 3 CAUSES YOU'D LIKE TO GET MORE INVOLVED WITH?

_____

_____

_____

_____

_____

_____

_____

_____

_____

_____

_____

_____

DATE: ___/___/20___

THINK ABOUT THE LAST TIME YOU WERE ALONE IN A CROWD.

WHAT WAS IT LIKE?

_____

_____

_____

_____

_____

_____

_____

_____

_____

_____

_____

Some people experience "spring fever" as being excited, agitated, and awake.

HOW WOULD YOU CHARACTERIZE YOUR MOOD RIGHT NOW? WHAT'S SCARY, LIBERATING, OR WEIRD ABOUT THE WAY YOU'RE FEELING?

_____

_____

_____

_____

_____

_____

_____

_____

_____

YOU'RE FLOATING IN A LAKE, LOOKING INTO THE SKY, FLOWER PETALS TICKLING YOUR FINGERS AND TOES.

IF YOUR BEST FRIEND COULD SEE YOU RIGHT NOW, HOW WOULD THEY ANALYZE YOUR BEHAVIOR?

_____

_____

_____

_____

_____

_____

_____

_____

David Lynch makes a movie about the last three years of your life.

WRITE ABOUT THE MAIN CHARACTERS AS SEEN THROUGH HIS EYES.

_____

_____

_____

_____

_____

_____

_____

IF YOU COULD LIVE INSIDE ONE BOOK, WHAT WOULD IT BE AND WHY?

DATE: ___/___/20___

WHEN WAS THE LAST TIME YOU DID SOMETHING REALLY NICE FOR YOURSELF?

FOR SOMEONE ELSE? WHEN WAS THE LAST TIME YOU FELT
APPRECIATED FOR BEING EXACTLY WHO YOU ARE?

_____

_____

_____

_____

_____

_____

_____

_____

_____

Today, your life is a Sam Cooke song.

WHAT ARE THE LYRICS?

_____

_____

_____

_____

_____

_____

_____

_____

_____

_____

THINK ABOUT THE LAST TIME YOU FELT JUDGED, DEVALUED, OR JUST RESTLESS.

WHAT ARE THE 5 WORDS YOU WOULD USE TO DESCRIBE THE EXPERIENCE?

_____

_____

_____

_____

_____

_____

_____

WHAT'S YOUR ULTIMATE REVENGE FANTASY? WRITE A SHORT PARAGRAPH DESCRIBING IT.

_____

_____

_____

_____

_____

_____

_____

_____

WHICH CITY IN THE WORLD FEELS MOST LIKE HOME TO YOU AND WHY?

DATE: ___/___/20___

There's a knock on your door. You open it and discover a wicker basket with a note in it.

YOU'RE INVITED ON A HOT-AIR BALLOON RIDE, WHICH LIFTS OFF FROM YOUR ROOF AND DROPS YOU DOWN IN THE CARIBBEAN. ONE HISTORICAL FIGURE CAN ACCOMPANY YOU. WHO DO YOU INVITE?

_____

_____

_____

_____

_____

_____

_____

DATE: ___/___/20___

WHAT TIME OF DAY IS MOST INSPIRING TO YOU?

WHAT TIME IS LONELIEST?

_____

_____

_____

_____

_____

_____

_____

_____

_____

_____

WHAT IS THE MOST IMPORTANT LESSON YOU'VE LEARNED RECENTLY?

_____

_____

_____

_____

_____

_____

_____

_____

_____

_____

"I'll throw off my sorrow / Beg, steal or borrow / My share of laughter."

"WHO CAN I TURN TO?" ⚡ TONY BENNETT

WHO OR WHAT DOES THIS QUOTE REMIND YOU OF?

_____

_____

_____

_____

_____

_____

_____

_____

_____

DATE: __/__/20__

IT'S SPRING
BUT IT'S ALMOST
SUMMER.

WHAT'S YOUR BIGGEST HOPE FOR THE NEXT FEW MONTHS?

_____

_____

_____

_____

_____

_____

_____

_____

_____

_____

_____

IF SPRING WERE A SPICE OR A SCENT THIS YEAR, WHAT WAS IT?

BLACK PEPPER, CURRY, ANISE, ROSEMARY, LAVENDER?

_____

_____

_____

_____

_____

_____

_____

I love you
for sentimental
reasons.

WHAT ARE THEY?

_____

_____

_____

_____

_____

_____

_____

_____

_____

_____

_____

ROSES ARE RED, VIOLETS ARE BLUE...

(FINISH THE POEM.)

_____

_____

_____

_____

_____

_____

_____

_____

_____

_____

_____

DATE: __ /__/20__

The birth of Venus.
The birth of you.

HOW ARE YOU ABOUT TO BLOOM?

_____

_____

_____

_____

_____

_____

_____

_____

_____

_____

_____

DATE: ___/___/20___

YOU KNOW THAT ALBUM YOU KEEP HEARING IS STRAIGHT FIRE FROM YOUR FRIENDS.

LISTEN TO IT WITH YOUR EYES CLOSED, IN YOUR BED.
WRITE DOWN 5 THINGS IT MAKES YOU FEEL.

_____

_____

_____

_____

_____

_____

Put your phone on "do not disturb" mode and look at your closet. Make a pile of things to donate or sell. Don't be sentimental.

WRITE DOWN ONE MEMORY THAT ONE PIECE OF CLOTHING CONJURES UP.

_____

_____

_____

_____

_____

_____

_____

Think of summer: ripe fruit, ice cream melting and dripping onto the sidewalk, your feet in sandals.

WRITE DOWN 3 MEMORIES YOU HAVE FROM LAST SUMMER THAT ARE TRULY MAGICAL, AND WRITE DOWN 3 WISHES YOU HAVE FOR THIS ONE.

DATE: ___ / ___ /20___

WHAT 3 SONGS JUST FEEL LIKE SUMMER TO YOU?

BECAUSE YOU...

A) GOT STONED LISTENING TO THEM IN HIGH SCHOOL.
B) DISCOVERED THEM AT A DRIVE-IN MOVIE THEATER.
C) JUST GET BUTTERFLIES WHEN THEY COME ON OVER THE
   SPEAKERS AT THE BEACH.

_____

_____

_____

_____

_____

_____

_____

WRITE DOWN 3 THINGS YOU ENVISION FRIDA KAHLO DOING WITH DIEGO RIVERA AT THEIR HOME IN MEXICO.

AND THEN CALL A FRIEND TO DO ONE OF THEM.

_____

_____

_____

_____

_____

_____

_____

_____

_____

DATE: ___ /___/20___

CUT TO PATRICK SWAYZE (IN THAT INCREDIBLE LEATHER JACKET) SAYING, "NOBODY PUTS BABY IN THE CORNER."

THEN WRITE DOWN YOUR 3 "BREAKOUT" MOMENTS FOR SUMMER—THINGS YOU WANT TO DO TO SURPRISE YOURSELF, PARENTS, OR FRIENDS. (AND IF THAT'S A SLAMMIN' DANCE NUMBER, WE'RE TOTALLY GOOD WITH IT.)

_____

_____

_____

_____

_____

_____

_____

_____

_____

"I NEVER DREAMED YOU'D LEAVE IN SUMMER / I THOUGHT YOU WOULD GO THEN COME BACK HOME / I THOUGHT THE COLD WOULD LEAVE BY SUMMER / BUT MY QUIET NIGHTS WILL BE SPENT ALONE."

IS ANYONE BETTER THAN STEVIE WONDER? WRITE DOWN YOUR MOST HEARTBREAKING SUMMER MEMORY, THE ONE THAT MAKES YOU CLIMB UNDER YOUR SHEETS. WHY IS IT STICKING WITH YOU AND HOW CAN YOU LET IT GO?

_____

_____

_____

_____

DATE: ___/___/20___

Grab some friends, a picnic blanket, and your favorite grapes and cheeses. Go to the nearest park.

OPEN THIS PAGE AND WRITE DOWN THE SMELLS ALL AROUND YOU: THE GRASS, THE BEER SPILLED ON THE SIDEWALK, THE BURGERS. AND THEN WRITE DOWN YOUR FAVORITE SUMMER SMELLS—THE ONES THAT LEAVE YOU TINGLING ALL YEAR LONG.

_____

_____

_____

_____

_____

DATE: ___/___/20___

"I tried with you / There's more to life than sleeping in and getting high with you / I had to let go of us to show myself what I could do / And that just didn't sit right with you."

A QUOTE FROM EVERYONE'S FAVORITE CANADIAN, DRAKE. WRITE DOWN A PAINFUL MEMORY FROM YOUR LAST BREAKUP. WHAT DID IT TEACH YOU? HOW ARE YOU EMPOWERED TO MOVE ON AND BE BIGGER AND BETTER THAN EVER BEFORE?

_____

_____

_____

_____

_____

_____

_____

DATE: ___ /___/20___

Take this journal up to a roof—yours or a friend's, doesn't matter. Look up at the sky and envision this landscape, 50 years ago.

WHAT WAS DIFFERENT? WHAT IS THE SAME? WHAT'S YOUR FAVORITE THING ABOUT BEING UP HERE?

_____

_____

_____

_____

_____

_____

_____

_____

DATE: ___/___/20___

LOOK UP THE NEAREST SPOT FOR BLUEBERRY PICKING.

CALL YOUR FRIEND—THE ONE WHO IS ALWAYS DOWN FOR A ROAD TRIP—AND HEAD TO YOUR DESTINATION. ONCE YOU'RE SLAPHAPPY FROM SUMMER SUN AND BERRY JUICE, WRITE DOWN YOUR BIGGEST WISH FOR THE SUMMER. FRIENDSHIP, ROMANCE, INSPIRATION, PHILANTHROPY—WHAT ARE YOU GOING TO MAKE HAPPEN FOR YOURSELF?

_____

_____

_____

_____

_____

_____

DATE: ___/___/20___

Take yourself on a date to the nearest farmer's market.

APPROACH EACH STALL LIKE YOU'RE JULIA CHILD. PICK ONLY THE FRUITS, VEGGIES, JAMS, AND BUTTERS THAT SEEM KINDA ORGASMICALLY DELICIOUS. BUY $20 WORTH, NO MORE, NO LESS. INVITE SOMEONE OVER FOR DINNER (OR AT LEAST DESSERT). WRITE DOWN YOUR MENU HERE.

_____

_____

_____

_____

_____

_____

_____

DATE: __/__/20__

"ALL MOVEMENT IS A DEEPENING TOWARD BRAVERY, TOWARD LOVE IF YOU ARE WILLING TO CARRY ITS NAME IN LIGHT."

⚡ COLLEEN HAMILTON-LECKY

WHAT'S THE LAST THING YOU DID THAT MADE YOU FEEL REALLY BRAVE?

_____

_____

_____

_____

_____

_____

_____

DATE: ___/___/20___

Envision yourself in Greece, standing at the edge of a steep cliff, about to dive into the endless blue below.

WHAT ONE THOUGHT WOULD GO THROUGH YOUR MIND?
A REVELATION, AN ANXIETY, A FAVORITE PERSON?

_____

_____

_____

_____

_____

_____

_____

_____

DATE: ___/___/20___

"I HAVE WORK, AND THEN I HAVE A DINNER THING, AND THEN I AM BUSY TRYING TO BECOME WHO I AM."

⚡ HANNAH HORVATH IN *GIRLS*

WHO ARE YOU BUSY TRYING TO BECOME THIS WEEK?

_____

_____

_____

_____

_____

_____

Get on the train. Get off at a stop you've never visited before. Walk around for 20 minutes, an hour if you've got it.

IF YOU WERE WRITING THE SCREENPLAY OF THIS MOMENT, WHAT WOULD YOU SAY?

_____

_____

_____

_____

_____

_____

_____

_____

_____

_____

DATE: ___/___/20___

Think about the grandparent you are or were the closest to. Think of their face, their hands, their advice.

WHAT IS THE SINGLE LINE YOU'D USE TO DESCRIBE THEM? AND WHAT IS ONE THING YOU'VE LEARNED FROM THEM?

_____

_____

_____

_____

_____

_____

_____

_____

DATE: ___/___/20___

You get 20 minutes trapped in the closet with Ryan Gosling.

WRITE DOWN WHAT HAPPENS.

_____

_____

_____

_____

_____

_____

_____

_____

_____

_____

_____

YOU GET 20 MINUTES IN THE CLOSET WITH DONALD TRUMP.

WRITE DOWN WHAT HAPPENS.

_____

_____

_____

_____

_____

_____

_____

_____

_____

_____

_____

_____

_____

DATE: ___/___/20___

Flip through a cookbook you own but have never used.

SKIP TO PAGE 27. MAKE THAT RECIPE. WRITE DOWN
THE RESULTS.

_____

_____

_____

_____

_____

_____

_____

_____

WRITE DOWN ONE HOBBY YOU'VE DEVELOPED IN THE LAST YEAR.

WRITE DOWN ONE THING THAT HOBBY HAS TAUGHT YOU.

_____

_____

_____

_____

_____

_____

_____

_____

_____

DATE: ___/___/20___

Listen to "Madiba Riddim" by Drake, like now.

DANCE AROUND YOUR KITCHEN FOR A FEW MINUTES, THEN
COME BACK AND WRITE DOWN YOUR 3 FAVORITE SUMMER
MEMORIES (OF ALL TIME).

_____

_____

_____

_____

_____

_____

_____

_____

_____

_____

"WHAT A CAMERA LIKES ARE EYES WHICH HAVE LIFE AND TELL A STORY."

⚡ JEREMY IRONS

TELL THE STORY OF THE LAST PAIR OF EYES YOU FOUND RIVETING.

_____

_____

_____

_____

_____

_____

_____

DATE: __/__/20__

Listen to "Step by Step" by Whitney Houston. Sing loudly.

MAKE A PROMISE TO YOURSELF FOR THIS SUMMER, AND
WRITE DOWN THE FIRST STEP.

_____

_____

_____

_____

_____

_____

_____

_____

_____

DATE: ___/___/20___

"I DON'T REALLY LOOK LIKE PEOPLE IN FILMS; I LOOK LIKE PEOPLE IN PAINTINGS."

⚡ TILDA SWINTON

WRITE DOWN ONE PIECE OF ART YOU'D LIKE TO PAINT YOURSELF INTO.

_____

_____

_____

_____

_____

_____

_____

_____

_____

WRITE DOWN
THE ONE THING YOU
WOULD GET TATTOOED
ON YOUR BODY.

OR IF YOU HAVE ONE OR SEVERAL, PICK YOUR FAVORITE TATTOO AND TELL ITS STORY.

_____

_____

_____

_____

_____

_____

_____

_____

_____

DATE: __ /__/20__

EAT A
VANILLA SUNDAE.

DESCRIBE THE PERFECT LICK.

DATE: __/__/20__

When was the last time you had sex with someone you really wanted?

DID TIME SLOW? WHAT MADE THE ENCOUNTER SO STEAMY?

_____

_____

_____

_____

_____

_____

_____

_____

_____

_____

"And so with the sunshine and the great bursts of leaves growing on the trees, just as things grow in fast movies, I had that familiar conviction that life was beginning over again with the summer."

FROM *THE GREAT GATSBY* ⚡ BY F. SCOTT FITZGERALD

WRITE DOWN ONE THING YOU'RE OPTIMISTIC ABOUT.

_____

_____

_____

_____

_____

_____

YOU COME BACK TO LIFE AS A PIECE OF RIPE FRUIT.

DESCRIBE IT IN 3 SENTENCES.

In 2017, Nike designed its Pro Hijab, which may empower a whole generation of women to compete for the world's highest medals.

WRITE DOWN 3 THINGS YOU'D LIKE TO ACHIEVE OF THAT MAGNITUDE.

_____

_____

_____

_____

_____

_____

_____

_____

_____

_____

DATE: ___ /___/20___

TODAY, YOU'RE ONE OF FAST COMPANY'S 100 MOST CREATIVE PEOPLE.

WHAT IS YOUR INVENTION, CONTRIBUTION, ACHIEVEMENT? AND WHO DOES IT BENEFIT?

_____

_____

_____

_____

_____

_____

_____

_____

"And love is a curse / Shoved in a hearse / Love is an open book to a verse / Of your bad poetry."

"I CAN CHANGE" ⚡ LCD SOUNDSYSTEM

WHAT'S THE CHEESIEST THING YOU'VE EVER THOUGHT ABOUT LOVE OR A LOVER?

_____

_____

_____

_____

_____

_____

_____

Today, you own a dance hall in Jamaica.

WHAT IS IT CALLED? WHO ARE YOUR REGULARS?

_____

_____

_____

_____

_____

_____

_____

_____

_____

_____

TODAY, YOU'RE A JAZZ SAXOPHONIST LIVING IN NEW ORLEANS.

WHAT'S YOUR FAVORITE VENUE? WHAT IS YOUR
SIGNATURE SONG?

_____

_____

_____

_____

_____

_____

_____

_____

_____

_____

DATE: __ /__/20__

YOU'RE DESIGNING A LIMITED EDITION PAIR OF HIGH-FASHION SNEAKERS.

HOW DO THEY LOOK? WHICH COUNTRY DO THEY GAIN INSANE POPULARITY IN?

_____

_____

_____

_____

_____

_____

_____

_____

_____

_____

You win the Nobel Peace Prize.

WHAT IS IT FOR?

_____

_____

_____

_____

_____

_____

_____

_____

_____

_____

_____

What's your favorite song from 1980s?

_____

_____

_____

_____

_____

_____

_____

_____

_____

_____

_____

_____

_____

_____

No matter where you are, imagine yourself on a fire escape, overlooking a little garden.

WHO IS HAVING A BEER AMID THE FLOWERS? DESCRIBE THE CHARACTERS.

_____

_____

_____

_____

_____

_____

_____

_____

_____

DATE: __/__/20__

YOU CHARTER A SAILBOAT AND TAKE OFF FOR 3 WEEKS OF TRAVEL.

WHERE ARE YOU HEADED AND WHY? WHAT'S WAITING
THERE FOR YOU?

_____

_____

_____

_____

_____

_____

_____

_____

_____

Describe the color you most associate with summer.

_____

_____

_____

_____

_____

_____

_____

_____

_____

_____

_____

_____

_____

Today, you're living inside a Sofia Coppola film.

WHAT ARE YOU WEARING? WHAT HAPPENS? DESCRIBE THE SETTING.

_____

_____

_____

_____

_____

_____

_____

_____

You're on the beach on Majorca, the waves licking the sand, a glass of sangria just inches away.

WHO IS NEXT TO YOU AND WHAT ARE YOU TALKING ABOUT?

_____

_____

_____

_____

_____

_____

BIGGIE OR TUPAC?

WHY?

_____

_____

_____

_____

_____

_____

_____

_____

_____

_____

_____

DATE: ___ / ___ /20___

SOFT SERVE OR ICE CREAM?

WHY?

_____

_____

_____

_____

_____

_____

_____

_____

_____

_____

_____

_____

_____

_____

DATE: __/__/20__

Cherries or melon?

WHY?

"A true friend is the one who holds your hand and touches your heart."

⚡ GABRIEL GARCÍA MÁRQUEZ

WHO IS THAT PERSON FOR YOU?

_____

_____

_____

_____

_____

_____

_____

_____

DESCRIBE THE LAST STRANGER YOU MET WHO REALLY INTRIGUED YOU.

_____

_____

_____

_____

_____

_____

_____

_____

_____

_____

_____

WHAT HAPPENED THE LAST TIME YOU WERE ON A ROOF?

DATE: ___ / ___ /20___

SUMMERTIME SADNESS IS A REAL THING.

WRITE ABOUT THE LAST THING THAT BROKE YOUR HEART
(EVEN IF IT WAS MOMENTARY).

_____

_____

_____

_____

_____

_____

_____

_____

_____

_____

SPEND 10 MINUTES LOOKING AT IMAGES FROM THE PHOTOGRAPHER GARRY WINOGRAND.

THEN WRITE A SHORT STORY BASED ON YOUR FAVORITE IMAGE.

_____

_____

_____

_____

_____

_____

_____

DATE: ___/___/20___

Which countries do you most want to visit?

WRITE A SENTENCE ABOUT WHY YOU WANT TO VISIT EACH
OF THEM. AFTER YOU'VE VISITED, FLIP BACK TO THIS PAGE
AND WRITE DOWN HOW YOUR IMPRESSIONS WERE
DIFFERENT FROM THE REALITY OF THE PLACE.

_____

_____

_____

_____

_____

_____

_____

_____

_____

WHAT DOES THE ICE CREAM TRUCK'S SONG MAKE YOU THINK OF?

_____

_____

_____

_____

_____

_____

_____

_____

_____

_____

_____

DATE: ___/___/20___

The ultimate beach song is Janet Jackson's "When I Think of You."

DISAGREE? WHAT'S YOURS?

_____

_____

_____

_____

_____

_____

_____

DATE: ___ /___/20___

You know that scene in *Girls*, when Elijah is singing "Cool for the Summer" through the wall to Hannah?

AND IT'S KINDA HEARTBREAKING BUT ON THE MONEY?
THINK OF YOUR LAST HEAT WAVE HEARTBREAK.
WHAT HAPPENED?

_____

_____

_____

_____

_____

_____

_____

_____

_____

_____

DATE: ___/___/20___

You fall from heaven into a bucket of summer berries.

DESCRIBE THE REST OF THIS SATURDAY NIGHT.

_____

_____

_____

_____

_____

_____

_____

_____

_____

_____

SOMETIMES PLACES IN THE SUMMER FEEL TINY. SOMETIMES THEY FEEL ENDLESS.

WHICH IS IT RIGHT NOW?

_____

_____

_____

_____

_____

_____

_____

_____

_____

_____

DATE: __/__/20__

SOMETIMES IN THE SUMMER I LIKE TO...

(FILL IN THE BLANK WITH YOUR FAVORITE HABITS.)

_____

_____

_____

_____

_____

_____

_____

_____

_____

_____

DATE: ___/___/20___

BEST PART
ABOUT SUMMER
RAINSTORMS?

_____

_____

_____

_____

_____

_____

_____

_____

_____

_____

_____

Worst part about sweating all month long?

_____

_____

_____

_____

_____

_____

_____

_____

_____

_____

DATE: ___ /___/20___

LISTEN TO JULIETTE GRÉCO FOR 5 MINUTES.

WRITE DOWN WHERE YOUR BRAIN GOES DURING THE EXPERIENCE.

_____

_____

_____

_____

_____

_____

_____

_____

_____

_____

_____

_____

Everything feels a little restless this time of year.

WHAT ARE YOU GRAPPLING WITH RIGHT NOW?

_____

_____

_____

_____

_____

_____

_____

_____

TODAY, YOU LIVE INSIDE A SLIM AARONS PHOTOGRAPH.

WHAT IS YOUR LIFE LIKE?

_____

_____

_____

_____

_____

_____

_____

_____

DATE: ___/___/20___

"DAYDREAMS OF HOW WE USED TO BE..."

"MISS U" ⚡ BIGGIE SMALLS

WHO OR WHAT ARE YOU DAYDREAMING ABOUT?

_____

_____

_____

_____

_____

_____

_____

_____

_____

DATE: ___/___/20___

Where is your happy place?

_____

_____

_____

_____

_____

_____

_____

_____

_____

_____

_____

_____

DATE: ___/___/20___

WHAT EPIDEMIC/ SERIOUS WORLD ISSUE WOULD YOU MOST LIKE TO SOLVE?

WRITE DOWN 3 STEPS THAT WOULD WORK TOWARD ERADICATING IT.

_____

_____

_____

_____

_____

_____

_____

MARTINI– SHAKEN OR STIRRED?

WHY?

_____

_____

_____

_____

_____

_____

_____

_____

_____

_____

DATE: ___ / ___ /20___

YOU'RE THE MASTER OF YOUR OWN UNIVERSE.

WHAT'S THE BEST THING ABOUT THAT?

_____

_____

_____

_____

_____

_____

_____

_____

_____

_____

WHO DO YOU CURRENTLY WANT TO PUNT OFF THE SIDE OF A CLIFF?

BOSS, BROTHER, EX-BOYFRIEND?

_____

_____

_____

_____

_____

_____

_____

_____

Describe your perfect romantic love.

_____

_____

_____

_____

_____

_____

_____

_____

_____

_____

DATE: ___/___/20___

DESCRIBE YOUR PERFECT SUMMER NIGHT.

_____

_____

_____

_____

_____

_____

_____

_____

_____

_____

DATE: ___/___/20___

MADONNA IN THE '80S: ANGER, LACE, UNREQUITED LOVE, PASSION.

YOU RIGHT NOW:

_____

_____

_____

_____

_____

_____

_____

_____

_____

_____

WHAT SINGLE QUOTE FEELS MOST LIKE SUMMER TO YOU?

_____

_____

_____

_____

_____

_____

_____

_____

_____

_____

_____

_____

_____

What single sound is summer to you?

_____

_____

_____

_____

_____

_____

_____

_____

_____

_____

_____

_____

_____

_____

What was the best summer of your childhood like?

_____

_____

_____

_____

_____

_____

_____

_____

_____

_____

_____

_____

_____

HOW WOULD YOU CHARACTERIZE THIS WEEK FROM A FILM GENRE STANDPOINT?

COMEDY, TRAGEDY, NOIR, MOCKUMENTARY?

_____

_____

_____

_____

_____

_____

_____

_____

_____

_____

Summer lightning strikes your home and sends it rocketing across the country.

YOU LAND THREE STATES AWAY, PLOPPING DOWN INTO A
SUNFLOWER FIELD. WHAT HAPPENS NEXT?

_____

_____

_____

_____

_____

_____

_____

_____

_____

IF IT'S HOT AF RIGHT NOW: THINK ABOUT THE COOLEST PLACE ON PLANET EARTH.

DESCRIBE IT.

_____

_____

_____

_____

_____

_____

_____

DATE: ___/___/20___

IF IT'S THUNDER-STORMING RIGHT NOW: THINK ABOUT THE WETTEST PLACE ON EARTH.

DESCRIBE IT.

_____

_____

_____

_____

_____

_____

_____

DATE: ___/___/20___

MEDITATE ON THE IMAGE OF A CANDELABRA IN A GARDEN SOMEWHERE.

WHAT DOES THE LIGHT LOOK LIKE? WHO IS SITTING IN THE GRASS?

_____

_____

_____

_____

_____

_____

DATE: __/__/20__

Whether you know it, you're lovely for many reasons.

TRY TO DESCRIBE HOW BEING LOVELY FEELS.

_____
_____
_____
_____
_____
_____
_____
_____

What's your definition of hospitality?

_____

_____

_____

_____

_____

_____

_____

_____

_____

_____

SOMEWHERE IN THE DISTANCE A GUY IS PLAYING AN ELECTRIC CELLO.

WHAT DO THE FIRST FEW NOTES REMIND YOU OF?

_____

_____

_____

_____

_____

_____

DATE: ___/___/20___

WHERE IS YOUR FIRST LOVE?

WRITE A 3-LINE POEM ABOUT YOUR RELATIONSHIP.

_____

_____

_____

_____

_____

_____

_____

_____

_____

A DOG NAMED CAESAR SHOWS UP AT YOUR DOOR.

HE BARKS, HE JUMPS INTO YOUR BED, HE READS THE NEWSPAPER. HE HAS A MAGICAL TALENT YOU WISH YOU HAD. WHAT IS IT?

_____

_____

_____

_____

_____

_____

_____

_____

_____

_____

DATE: ___/___/20

ENVISION YOUR LIFE 2 DAYS FROM NOW, 1 WEEK, 8 YEARS.

WHAT DO YOU HOPE IS EXACTLY THE SAME?

_____

_____

_____

_____

_____

_____

YOU INHERIT AN OLIVE OIL FARM IN ORTYGIA, SICILY.

YOU RUN AWAY AND LIVE THERE IN SOLITUDE FOR A DECADE. WHEN YOU COME BACK, WHAT ABOUT YOUR LIFE HAS CHANGED? WHAT IS THE SAME?

_____

_____

_____

_____

_____

_____

_____

_____

_____

ARE YOU READY FOR HEAVEN?

WHAT'S YOUR FAVORITE SMITHS LYRIC?

_____

_____

_____

_____

_____

_____

_____

_____

_____

_____

_____

_____

DATE: ___/___/20___

THIS MOMENT IS RACING THROUGH YOUR FINGERS, LIKE HORSES OUTTA THE STABLE.

WHAT DO YOU HOPE TO ALWAYS REMEMBER ABOUT RIGHT NOW?

_____

_____

_____

_____

_____

_____

_____

DATE: __ / __ /20

YOUR LIFE IS SO BEAUTIFUL.

SAY MORE ABOUT THAT.

_____

_____

_____

_____

_____

_____

_____

_____

_____

_____

If you were to drive around with your windows down, a bandanna in your hair and a song booming out to wake everyone up, what would it be?

_____

_____

_____

_____

_____

_____

_____

_____

_____

DATE: __ /__/20__

"DON'T THINK / IT COMPLICATES THINGS / JUST FEEL, AND / IF IT FEELS LIKE HOME / THEN FOLLOW / ITS PATH."

"FIND YOUR PATHS" ⚡ R. M. DRAKE

WHAT'S ONE THING THAT FEELS LIKE HOME THAT YOU
WANT TO WRITE ABOUT? DESCRIBE IT IN 3 SENTENCES.

_____

_____

_____

_____

DATE: ___ /___/20___

"WHAT / WE SPEAK / BECOMES THE HOUSE WE LIVE IN."

⚡ HAFIZ

WRITE DOWN 3 ASPIRATIONS YOU HAVE FOR YOUR LIFE.

_____

_____

_____

_____

_____

_____

DATE: __/__/20__

"Ultimately, my hope is to amaze myself."

⚡ JERRY UELSMANN

WRITE DOWN 3 THINGS YOUR FRIENDS DO FOR YOU THAT AMAZE YOU, AND WRITE DOWN 3 THINGS YOU WANT TO DO IN RETURN FOR THEM.

DATE: ___/___/20___

"They said that it's her time, no tears in sight, I kept the feelings close / And you took hold of me and never, never, never let me go / 'Cause no one knows me like the piano in my mother's home / In my mother's home."

"(NO ONE KNOWS ME)LIKE THE PIANO" ⚡ SAMPHA

VISUALIZE THE OBJECT THAT REALLY MEANS SOMETHING TO YOU IN A HOME—YOURS, YOUR BROTHER'S, YOUR PARENTS'. WHAT IS IT ABOUT THAT OBJECT THAT TOUCHES YOUR SECRET LITTLE SOUL?

_____

_____

_____

DATE: __ /__ /20__

Fall—it's time for a good shearling jacket and some wonderfully sentimental feels.

WRITE DOWN YOUR 3 FAVORITE THINGS ABOUT THIS TIME OF YEAR.

_____

_____

_____

_____

_____

_____

_____

_____

_____

_____

TODAY, YOU'RE A 35MM CAMERA.

IT'S YOUR JOB TO SEE BEAUTY AND LIGHT, SHADOWS AND SATURATION. WHEN TODAY IS DONE, COME BACK HERE AND WRITE DOWN THE MOST MAGICAL THING YOU WITNESSED.

_____

_____

_____

_____

_____

_____

_____

_____

_____

_____

TODAY, YOU'RE A RADIO HOST.

YOU ASK QUESTIONS, INQUIRE FOR MORE INFORMATION, COAX STORIES OUT OF EVERYONE YOU MEET. WHAT IS THE BEST ONE-LINER YOU RECEIVE?

DATE: ___ /___/20___

"IT IS THE GREATEST OF ALL MISTAKES TO DO NOTHING BECAUSE YOU CAN ONLY DO A LITTLE. DO WHAT YOU CAN."

⚡ SYDNEY SMITH

WRITE DOWN 3 SMALL THINGS YOU CAN DO TO BE HELPFUL. WATERING A NEIGHBOR'S PLANT? BABYSITTING? DONATING BOOKS? DO ONE OF THE THINGS THIS WEEK.

_____

_____

_____

_____

_____

_____

DATE: __/__/20__

You know that animal shelter, the one you always pass on your way to the movies, the grocery store, your aunt's apartment?

OFFER TO VOLUNTEER THERE NEXT WEEKEND.
WRITE DOWN 3 LINES ABOUT THE EXPERIENCE.

_____

_____

_____

_____

_____

_____

_____

_____

DATE: ___ /___/20___

Go out of your way for a treat.

A REALLY NICE GLASS OF WINE, A CHOCOLATE TORTE, A SWEATER YOU'VE BEEN WANTING. WRITE DOWN 3 SENSATIONS YOU HAVE RELATED TO SAID TREAT.

_____

_____

_____

_____

_____

_____

_____

_____

_____

_____

"I like to do things that I adore. It can't be in between. I really need to connect... Because it's not a job. It's almost like a faith or religion. Every time, I give a bit of my soul."

⚡ EVA GREEN

WRITE DOWN WHAT YOU WANT TO GIVE A LITTLE BIT OF YOURSELF TO.

_____

_____

_____

_____

_____

_____

"THIS IS AMERICA. PICK A JOB AND THEN BECOME THE PERSON THAT DOES IT."

⚡ BOBBIE BARRETT IN *MAD MEN*

WHAT'S YOUR DREAM JOB? AND HOW ARE YOU GOING TO GET IT?

_____

_____

_____

_____

_____

Go to a wine bar, a French one. Order a bottle that's a splurge by most standards.

WRITE DOWN THE SPICES, SCENTS, AND FRUITS YOU CAN TASTE. THEN READ THE DESCRIPTION ON THE BOTTLE. DOES IT CONFIRM OR CHANGE YOUR EXPERIENCE?

_____

_____

_____

_____

_____

_____

_____

_____

_____

"There was something wrong with her. She did not know what it was but there was something wrong with her. A hunger, a restlessness. An incomplete knowledge of herself. The sense of something farther away, beyond her reach."

FROM *AMERICANAH* ⚡ BY SHIMAMANDA NGOZI ADICHIE

WRITE DOWN HOW WELL YOU KNOW YOURSELF AND RATE IT ON A SCALE OF 1–10.

_____

_____

_____

_____

DATE: __/__/20__

TODAY, YOU'RE ANNA WINTOUR.

WRITE DOWN A DESCRIPTION OF YOUR MORNING
(WHAT YOU WEAR, WHAT YOU EAT, WHOM YOU CHAT
WITH). TOMORROW, LIVE OUT THE LIST YOU'VE CREATED.

_____

_____

_____

_____

_____

_____

_____

_____

_____

_____

DATE: ___/___/20___

Think about one issue— political, social, religious— that you don't understand. Spend 10 minutes (right now) googling to

Q   understand it better.

WRITE DOWN ONE THING YOU'VE LEARNED.

_____

_____

_____

_____

_____

_____

_____

DATE: ___/___/20___

"If your hair is done properly and you're wearing good shoes, you can get away with anything."

⚡ IRIS APFEL

WRITE DOWN ONE THING YOU'RE GOING TO GET AWAY WITH TODAY, TOMORROW, THIS FALL.

_____

_____

_____

_____

_____

_____

_____

DATE: ___/___/20___

THERE'S A MANILA ENVELOPE WAITING ON YOUR DOORSTEP.

WHAT'S IN IT? AND WHO IS IT FROM?

_____

_____

_____

_____

_____

_____

_____

_____

_____

_____

_____

WHAT'S YOUR HOROSCOPE? WHAT ABOUT YOUR ZODIAC SIGN MAKES YOU PROUD?

WHAT SUCKS ABOUT IT?

_____

_____

_____

_____

_____

_____

_____

What does wisdom mean to you?

_____

_____

_____

_____

_____

_____

_____

_____

_____

_____

DATE: ___ /___/20___

WHAT DOES LONELINESS MEAN TO YOU?

_____

_____

_____

_____

_____

_____

_____

_____

_____

_____

_____

_____

WHAT DOES GREAT SEX FEEL LIKE FOR YOU?

_____

_____

_____

_____

_____

_____

_____

_____

_____

_____

_____

_____

What does a crush look like for you?

_____

_____

_____

_____

_____

_____

_____

_____

_____

_____

_____

DATE: __ /__/20__

TAKE YOURSELF ON A CULINARY ADVENTURE— TO LITTLE ITALY FOR SOME MASCARPONE OR TO THE WATERFRONT NEAR YOUR HOUSE FOR AN ICE CREAM.

DESCRIBE YOUR PURCHASE AND THE MEMORIES IT CONJURES IN 3 SENTENCES.

_____

_____

_____

_____

_____

_____

DATE: ___/___/20___

YOUR LIFE DEPENDS ON YOU GETTING 2 PIERCINGS.

WHERE ARE THEY? AND WHY?

_____

_____

_____

_____

_____

_____

_____

_____

_____

_____

YOU START A BAND.

WHO IS IN IT? AND WHAT ARE YOU CALLED?
WHAT INSTRUMENT DO YOU PLAY?

_____

_____

_____

_____

_____

_____

_____

_____

_____

_____

_____

_____

DATE: __/__/20__

YOU'RE ASKED BY THE PRESIDENT TO LEAD A MISSION TO MARS.

WHO IS IN YOUR SPACESHIP AND WHY? YOU CAN BRING 3 OBJECTS—WHAT ARE THEY?

_____

_____

_____

_____

_____

_____

_____

_____

_____

_____

DATE: ___/___/20___

NAME ONE SMALL BUT MEANINGFUL LUXURY YOU'D LIKE IN YOUR LIFE.

FOR INSTANCE, A GARDEN SO YOU CAN CLIP FLOWERS FOR YOUR KITCHEN TABLE. YOUR TURN.

_____

_____

_____

_____

_____

_____

_____

_____

_____

_____

DATE: ___/___/20___

"THERE'S ONLY ONE
MICHAEL JORDAN."

⚡ MICHAEL JORDAN

THERE'S ONLY ONE YOU. DESCRIBE THE THINGS THAT ARE
EXQUISITE AND REAL ABOUT YOU AND YOU ALONE.

_____

_____

_____

_____

_____

_____

_____

_____

_____

_____

Who is your all-time favorite teacher and what did you learn from them?

_____

_____

_____

_____

_____

_____

_____

_____

_____

You're an anthropologist.

NOTICE THE PEOPLE AND PLACES YOU'RE MOVING
THROUGH: THE BUILDINGS, THE DOGS, THE TREES,
THE DIRT, THE LAUGHTER. WRITE DOWN THE 5 THINGS THAT
JUMP OUT AT YOU.

_____

_____

_____

_____

_____

_____

_____

_____

_____

_____

You invite Picasso over for dinner.

WHAT DO YOU COOK? WHAT DOES HE WEAR?
WHAT DO YOU DISCUSS?

_____

_____

_____

_____

_____

_____

_____

_____

_____

_____

_____

You set sail and discover a new country and plant a flag in the soil.

WHAT DOES THE FLAG LOOK LIKE? AND WHAT DO THE SYMBOLS REPRESENT?

_____

_____

_____

_____

_____

_____

_____

_____

_____

_____

_____

WHEN WAS THE LAST TIME YOU FELT TRULY POWERLESS?

DATE: __/__/20__

Have you ever had a sex dream about a friend?

WHO WAS IT AND WHAT HAPPENED?

_____

_____

_____

_____

_____

_____

_____

_____

_____

_____

_____

_____

DATE: ___/___/20__

YOU'RE PART OF A MAJOR MUSEUM HEIST.

WHAT PIECES OF ART DO YOU STEAL AND WHAT DO YOU
DO WITH YOUR STOLEN MILLIONS?

_____

_____

_____

_____

_____

_____

_____

_____

_____

_____

_____

_____

_____

What is your favorite fall dish?

_____

_____

_____

_____

_____

_____

_____

_____

_____

_____

_____

DATE: ___ /___ /20___

WRITE DOWN THE TITLE OF THE LAST SONG, POEM, EXHIBIT, OR INTERACTION THAT STAYED WITH YOU.

WHY WAS IT REMARKABLE?

_____

_____

_____

_____

_____

_____

_____

_____

_____

_____

_____

DATE: __ /__/20__

You wake up tomorrow as a plant, flower, or tree. Describe your surroundings, your colors, your scents.

WHO TOUCHES YOU, TALKS TO YOU, WATERS YOU?

_____

_____

_____

_____

_____

_____

_____

_____

TODAY, YOU'RE A MUSIC PRODUCER. WHAT'S THE STYLE THAT YOU'RE KNOWN FOR?

_____

_____

_____

_____

_____

_____

_____

_____

_____

_____

THINK ABOUT THE 3 JOBS YOU WOULD LEAST LIKE TO PERFORM.

WHAT IS IT ABOUT THEM THAT TURNS YOU OFF? AND DOES THAT MAKE YOU GRATEFUL FOR YOUR CURRENT POSITION IN ANY WAY?

_____

_____

_____

_____

_____

_____

_____

_____

_____

DATE: ___/___/20___

In some ways, fall feels like the beginning of everything— the world starting anew.

SET 3 INTENTIONS FOR THE SEASON.

_____

_____

_____

_____

_____

_____

_____

_____

_____

_____

_____

What's different from a year ago to now?

_____

_____

_____

_____

_____

_____

_____

_____

_____

_____

_____

_____

_____

_____

WHAT DO YOU THINK KATE MOSS IS DOING RIGHT NOW?

_____

_____

_____

_____

_____

_____

_____

_____

_____

_____

_____

YOU ARE HAVING LUNCH WITH ELIZABETH TAYLOR. WHAT ADVICE DOES SHE GIVE YOU?

_____

_____

_____

_____

_____

_____

_____

_____

_____

_____

_____

WHEN YOU WERE GROWING UP, WHAT WAS YOUR FAVORITE FALL TRADITION?

_____

_____

_____

_____

_____

_____

_____

_____

What is your favorite fall sweater like?

_____

_____

_____

_____

_____

_____

_____

_____

_____

_____

_____

Who do you miss the most today?

_____

_____

_____

_____

_____

_____

_____

_____

_____

_____

WHAT SECRET IS WEIGHING ON YOU RIGHT NOW?

What political topic is most pressing for you right now?

_____

_____

_____

_____

_____

_____

_____

_____

_____

Who was the last author that really changed your point of view?

SAY A FEW WORDS ABOUT WHY THEIR WRITING INFLUENCED YOU.

_____

_____

_____

_____

_____

_____

_____

_____

"A MAN SEES IN THE WORLD WHAT HE CARRIES IN HIS HEART."

⚡ GOETHE

HOW IS THAT TRUE OR NOT TRUE OF YOU?

_____

_____

_____

_____

_____

_____

_____

WHO IS YOUR FAVORITE CHARACTER FROM *THE SOPRANOS* AND WHY?

(IF YOU HAVEN'T SEEN IT,
USE THIS MOMENT TO WATCH THE PILOT.)

_____

_____

_____

_____

_____

_____

_____

_____

WHAT 5 SONGS WOULD DEFINITELY BE PART OF THE SOUNDTRACK TO YOUR LIFE?

TODAY, APPROACH THE WORLD LIKE YOU'RE ANSEL ADAMS, NATURE PHOTOGRAPHER.

WHAT IMAGES DO YOU CAPTURE?

_____

_____

_____

_____

_____

_____

_____

_____

_____

"Heaven help the child who never had a home / Heaven help the girl who walks the streets alone / Heaven help the roses if the bombs begin to fall / Heaven help us all."

"HEAVEN HELP US ALL" ⚡ STEVIE WONDER

WHO ARE YOU PRAYING FOR TODAY?

_____

_____

_____

_____

_____

_____

_____

DATE: __/__/20__

YOU TRADE LIVES WITH A GOAT HERDER IN ICELAND.

**WHAT'S THE BEST PART OF YOUR DAY?
WHAT DO YOU MISS THE MOST?**

_____

_____

_____

_____

_____

_____

_____

_____

DATE: ___/___/20___

Imagine you are a wool blanket on the first day of fall.

WRITE THE STORY OF BEING THAT BLANKET—THE PEOPLE YOU MEET, THE SONGS YOU HEAR, THE WAY THE LIGHT FEELS HITTING YOUR STRIPES AROUND 4 IN THE AFTERNOON.

_____

_____

_____

_____

_____

_____

DATE: ___ /___/20___

"I LIKE THE SMELL OF THE TRASH AND LEAVES / BURNING IN THE CANS / ROGER IS THE BOY NEXT DOOR, HE'S A WANDERER / HE STARTS WITH HIS HANDS."

"FINDLAY, OHIO 1968" ⚡ INDIGO GIRLS

WHO DOES ROGER REMIND YOU OF?

_____

_____

_____

_____

_____

_____

DATE: ___/___/20___

YOU FALL FROM HEAVEN, LANDING IN A GIANT PILE OF ORANGEY-AUBURN LEAVES.

WHAT HAPPENS NEXT IN THE HBO VERSION OF THIS STORY?

_____

_____

_____

_____

_____

_____

_____

_____

_____

Describe the 3 objects (edible, intangible, sensual) that most remind you of autumn.

_____

_____

_____

_____

_____

_____

_____

_____

_____

_____

_____

A RUSSIAN MASTER CREATES A BALLET OF YOUR LIFE, AND IT BEGINS IN OCTOBER.

WHAT ARE THE CHARACTERS' NAMES AND WHAT ARE THE 3 CRUCIAL PLOT TWISTS?

_____

_____

_____

_____

_____

_____

DATE: ___/___/20___

Life is but a dream.

WHEN WAS THE LAST TIME YOU FELT THAT WAS TRUE?

_____

_____

_____

_____

_____

_____

_____

_____

_____

_____

_____

_____

DESCRIBE A SUBLIME AUTUMN MOMENT FROM ANY POINT IN YOUR LIFE.

_____

_____

_____

_____

_____

_____

_____

DATE: __ / __ /20__

A STORYBOOK WITCH OFFERS YOU A BITE OF A GLISTENING, SLIGHTLY WAXY RED APPLE.

WHAT HAPPENS NEXT IS THE WORLD'S SCARIEST TALE.
WRITE IT.

_____

_____

_____

_____

_____

_____

_____

_____

Mick Jagger rolls up to your front door wearing a velvet suit. He asks if you'd like to join him for Thanksgiving.

WRITE THE EMAIL YOU'D SEND TO YOUR MOTHER AFTER THE FACT.

_____

_____

_____

_____

_____

_____

_____

_____

_____

_____

YOU GO APPLE PICKING WITH BIGGIE SMALLS IN RURAL CONNECTICUT.

WHAT IS MOST SURPRISING ABOUT THIS?

_____

_____

_____

_____

_____

_____

_____

_____

You open your eyes and find yourself next to Joan of Arc, a fire blazing to your right.

WRITE DOWN 10 WORDS THAT DESCRIBE WHAT HAPPENS NEXT.

_____

_____

_____

_____

_____

_____

_____

_____

DATE: __ /__/20__

THIS FALL,
YOU'RE INVINCIBLE.

YOU SCALE THE EIFFEL TOWER, THE STATUE OF LIBERTY.
ON THE BROOKLYN BRIDGE, YOU FALL THOUSANDS OF FEET
INTO THE ICY WATER BELOW, UNTOUCHED. WHO DO YOU
MEET WHEN YOU EMERGE ONTO THE HIGHWAY?

_____

_____

_____

_____

_____

_____

_____

_____

_____

_____

DATE: __ /__/20__

You commission Botticelli for a fall portrait of your favorite subject—fruit, vegetable, animal, whatever you like.

WHAT IS THE END RESULT?

_____

_____

_____

_____

_____

_____

_____

_____

_____

_____

_____

WHAT ARE YOU MOST FEARFUL OF?

What are you most hopeful for?

_____

_____

_____

_____

_____

_____

_____

_____

_____

_____

_____

_____

Today, your life is a Jerry Butler– Thelma Houston album.

WHAT ARE THE MAIN THEMES OF SAID ALBUM AND WHAT DOES THE COVER ART LOOK LIKE?

_____

_____

_____

_____

_____

_____

_____

_____

_____

_____

DATE: ___/___/20___

"THE FIRE THAT STIRS ABOUT HER, WHEN SHE STIRS..."

"THE FOLLY OF BEING COMFORTED" ⚡ W. B. YEATS

WHAT MAGIC HAVE YOU WITNESSED IN YOURSELF
OR SOMEONE ELSE LATELY?

WRITE ABOUT SOMETHING THAT THRILLS YOU.

_____

_____

_____

_____

_____

_____

_____

_____

_____

_____

_____

_____

_____

_____

_____

DATE: ___/___/20___

WRITE ABOUT SOMETHING THAT KILLS YOU.

_____

_____

_____

_____

_____

_____

_____

_____

WRITE ABOUT SOMETHING THAT IMPRESSES YOU.

_____

_____

_____

_____

_____

_____

_____

_____

_____

_____

_____

_____

WRITE ABOUT SOMETHING THAT HURTS YOU.

_____

_____

_____

_____

_____

_____

_____

_____

_____

_____

_____

_____

_____

DATE: __/__/20__

WHAT ARE YOUR CREATIVE GOALS FOR THIS YEAR?

_____

_____

_____

_____

_____

_____

_____

_____

_____

_____

_____

_____

_____

WHICH THOUGHT LEADERS ARE MOST IMPORTANT TO YOU RIGHT NOW?

DATE: __/__/20__

WRITE DOWN 5 PERSONAL PHILOSOPHIES YOU'VE DEVELOPED.

IF YOU DON'T HAVE ANY, TAKE 10 MINUTES TO THINK THROUGH ONE.

_____

_____

_____

_____

_____

_____

_____

What's your favorite jazz song, hip-hop anthem, classical composition?

_____

_____

_____

_____

_____

_____

_____

_____

THINK ABOUT A GOAL YOU'VE SET BUT HAVEN'T REACHED YET.

WRITE DOWN 3 STEPS THAT MIGHT HELP YOU GET THERE.

_____

_____

_____

_____

_____

_____

_____

_____

_____

What movie (or film, if we're going to be highbrow) has been most influential for you, and why?

DATE: ___/___/20___

"SHAKY AND I'M ON MY KNEES / THERE ARE BETTER THINGS FOR ME."

"DEADWATER" ⚡ WET

WHAT GREAT THINGS ARE YOU DESTINED FOR?

_____

_____

_____

_____

_____

_____

YOU WAKE UP AND KISS ALL YOUR INHIBITIONS GOOD-BYE.

WHAT HAPPENS NEXT?

_____

_____

_____

_____

_____

_____

_____

_____

_____

_____

_____

You're gifted with a month in Paris, free of charge, all experiences at your fingertips.

WHERE DO YOU GO? WHAT DO YOU SEE? WHAT DO YOU DO?

_____

_____

_____

_____

_____

_____

_____

THINK ABOUT ALL THE MYSTERIES OF THE UNIVERSE UNFOLDING BEFORE YOUR VERY EYES.

WHAT ARE THE FIRST 5 IMAGES THAT COME TO MIND?

_____

_____

_____

_____

_____

What is most precious to you?

BOOKS, FRIENDS, FAMILY, IDEAS, COLORS, PLACES? WRITE YOUR LITTLE HEART OUT ABOUT ALL OF THE ABOVE—THE THINGS THAT ARE KEEPING YOU HUNGRY, INSPIRED, AND RESILIENT.

_____

_____

_____

_____

_____

_____

_____

_____

_____

DATE: ___/___/20___

WHEN YOU DANCE, HOW DOES IT FEEL?

AND WHO IS YOUR FAVORITE PARTNER?

_____

_____

_____

_____

_____

_____

_____

_____

_____

_____

_____

_____

What had to end for you to begin?

_____

_____

_____

_____

_____

_____

_____

_____

_____